DUALITY

Krisha Anant

WESTBOW
PRESS®
A DIVISION OF THOMAS NELSON
& ZONDERVAN

Copyright © 2021 Krisha Anant.

All rights reserved. No part of this book may be used or reproduced by any means, graphic, electronic, or mechanical, including photocopying, recording, taping or by any information storage retrieval system without the written permission of the author except in the case of brief quotations embodied in critical articles and reviews.

This is a work of fiction. All of the characters, names, incidents, organizations, and dialogue in this novel are either the products of the author's imagination or are used fictitiously.

WestBow Press books may be ordered through booksellers or by contacting:

WestBow Press
A Division of Thomas Nelson & Zondervan
1663 Liberty Drive
Bloomington, IN 47403
www.westbowpress.com
844-714-3454

Because of the dynamic nature of the Internet, any web addresses or links contained in this book may have changed since publication and may no longer be valid. The views expressed in this work are solely those of the author and do not necessarily reflect the views of the publisher, and the publisher hereby disclaims any responsibility for them.

Any people depicted in stock imagery provided by Getty Images are models, and such images are being used for illustrative purposes only.
Certain stock imagery © Getty Images.

ISBN: 978-1-6657-0664-3 (sc)
ISBN: 978-1-6657-0665-0 (e)

Library of Congress Control Number: 2021911094

Print information available on the last page.

WestBow Press rev. date: 6/1/2021

CONTENTS

Heaven's Devil 1
I Can Become 2
Matryoshka Doll 3
A Helping Hand 4
The Sand of an Hourglass 5
Goodbye, Mother 7
Hopes and Wishes 8
Dear Human 9
Pockets 10
A Million Moments per Second 11
Can You See? 13
La Vida 14
Kitsune 15
The Nightingale's Song 17
Glass Hearts 18
Edge of Paradise 20
Evil Justice 21
Better Left Unsaid 22
The Space Between Their Hearts 23
Colorless Time 24
Fighting Without Fighting 26
All to Survive 27
If We Could Touch the Stars 28
Little Boy of the Woods 29
Chain Parade 30
Peaks 32

Shatter	33
Reflections in the Shards of Glass	34
Requiem for the Living	35
The Man Who Lives in 403B	36
The Same Souls	41
To Each City and Beyond	42
Worlds Away	43
Tomorrow	44
The Ashes of Our World	45
Little Cookie Girl	47
Tears of Blood	49
Silence	50
Redwood Winters	51
Big Fish	52
Hyacinths and Jasmine	54
Reach Across the Decades	55
Two Worlds	56
We Are Kings	57
Anywhere	58
The Only Loyalty	61
Quiet Outside	62
As Winter Comes and Goes	63
Love Yourself	65
Duality	66
About the Author	67

HEAVEN'S DEVIL

How may I match your beauty to the moon?
A moon too dim, held caged behind the clouds.
As inky night gives way to daylight's boon,
It lies in sorrow, abased to its shroud.
But thou fly free and high with abandon;
Hast thou no sky, nor a hell to fall to?
Thy movements, sharp as wind with intention,
Call me to dance, your lone duet for two.
Your silver lining glows whiter than white,
Shaming the moon, yellowed art of decay;
Thy rosy lips bloom slowly, smiles alight,
To entrance pure mortals, to lead astray.
Past time, as thou act immoral devil,
So long shall thou be immortal angel.

I CAN BECOME

Do not judge me for the shackles
Wrapped around my arms -
Do not dare to think we are still equals
And that I should always have no qualms.

Do not tell me I know not how to speak
When my mouth is bound and gagged -
Do not dare say that I am weak
When I was dragged through the mud till I was ragged.

Do not judge me for the smile that
Isn't on my face -
You never watched as someone spat
At you and called you a disgrace.

Judge me for my fearsome courage
And my beautiful, gentle soul -
Judge me for my message
And my hard work toward my goal.

Do not judge me for what I am today and call me loathsome -
Judge me for what is in my heart and what I can become.

MATRYOSHKA DOLL

The first layer is neutrality,
A rippling ocean of calm.
But if you look deeper in me,
You'll find my hidden charm.

Unscrew the outer dolly
To see the hate below;
Behold my anger, frustration and folly,
And the depths from which they flow.

Have you ever seen such carnage?
Did it make you fear me?
Still, if you have the courage,
Delve deeper into my memory.

For in the very last layer,
You find something of a brighter scope.
In the very last layer,
There is undiluted beauty and hope.

A HELPING HAND

"What does it mean to help?" she asks.
"I'll tell you," she hears as her neighbor joins.
"To help is to focus on yourself and your tasks."
And her neighbor leaves to count her pretty gold coins.

The girl still doesn't know what it means to help.
"I'll tell you what it means," her mother replies.
"You do what you're told without a complaint or a yelp."
And her mother leaves to finish chores and bake the pies.

"What does it mean to help?" she asks again.
"I'll tell you the truth", her friend confides.
"You must be virtuous and selfless - from vice, please refrain."
Her friend leaves with a gun and vile intentions -
from her conscience, she hides.

"What does it mean to help?" the girl asks.
This time, there is only silence.

THE SAND OF AN HOURGLASS

From the moment we awoke,
The desert was all we knew.
The sun's red rays a gentle stroke,
Each day began anew.

Oh! How we nursed our passions
In the fiery light of day
We gave no thought to our actions,
Cared not of what we'll pay.

For youth was all-encompassing,
And so we frolicked and played -
That time continued passing
Touched us only as we decayed.

And finally, we looked up and perceived
As the hollow light did pass -
That our whole lives were lived
In the sand of an hourglass.

GOODBYE, MOTHER

A tribute to the victims of the Sewol ferry incident

I'm leaving now, see you soon!

...See you soon indeed.

I left that morning with a skip in my step -
Do you remember? So entranced I was
with the thought of the sea,
That I could feel it calling out to me.

The ocean was perfect and pristine
(And sadistic and deadly)
And sparkled aquamarine with breathtaking beauty.

I meant every word of what I promised you
Though I could not know what it would mean.
This cruel fate operates unknown and unseen.

I saw you cry over dreams crushed and hopes gone -
I love you, and I left you, and for that I feel guilty.
I am sorry.

But a promise is a promise,
So please, on Earth, for a short while remain.
For in just some time, I will see you again.

Goodbye, Mother.

HOPES AND WISHES

The wishes are only pipe dreams
Stuck in the realm of fantasy -
Flitting by in unconscious streams,
They give only ecstasy.

But hopes are something tangible
And I hear their call in my soul -
With steps nearly invisible,
I may finally reach this goal.

But hoping takes courage,
And hoping takes force -
For if your resolve takes damage,
Then life might lose its course.

So believe that I won't lead you astray
When I talk of a life bedazzled -
Believe in my fortitude when I say
That I hope we can change the world.

DEAR HUMAN,

Did you think you could escape?
Is that why you ran
Until your feet bruised and your lungs ached?
Did you think your blind faith
Could save you from the hellfire
And your sinful fate?

Where were your neon gods
When you needed them the most?
No doubt, simply mocking your odds.
Where was your bravado
When you appeared at my door?
I'll give the benefit of doubt - maybe you were running low.

But you should know, dear human,
That we do not forgive or forget -
You can't simply shut the past behind the curtain.
So I welcome you to my land
And I wish you all the worst,
For this inferno is under my command.

Love,
Satan

POCKETS

These pockets from my old red coat
Have grown full and heavy -
Each one a special memory
Bringing me back to how things used to be.

The squashed paper crane in the right -
I would fold these carefully on my table in the kitchen
While mother made fresh pasta, delicious and seasoned,
And laughter colored the whole room innocently golden.

The four copper pennies in the left
I would find as I walked with father through town.
He would smile at my excitement and crouch down
As I showed him how I caught luck, tiny and brown.

And in the pocket closest to my heart
Is the charm of my very own angel;
When I doubt or fear the novel,
I feel its familiarity, warm and gentle.

Now I empty this coat and give it anew
To the next little girl to wrap herself in;
And if she ever finds herself in chagrin,
She can take comfort in these pockets, and the memories within.

A MILLION MOMENTS PER SECOND

My conscious mind cannot deny
How sometimes life just flutters by.
In a tick of a clock - in the blink of an eye,
There are a million moments per second.

And when I pause to look behind
A million moments leave me blind.
A trick of the mind - an instinct unrefined,
There are a million moments per second.

Sometimes I fear, sometimes I hate
This mad dash towards my fate -
The race of my life - the pounding of feet,
There are a million moments per second.

But when time does flow syrupy slow,
And leaves my memory fallow,
I know to look and appreciate the thrill
Of a million moments per second.

CAN YOU SEE?

Can you see the pixies
As they twirl to the ground?
Their twinkling wings beat joyously
And their sweet laughter echoes all around.

(Or do you only see the autumn leaves
and sigh at the coming winter?)

Can you see the dandelion puffs
As they float away to Neverland?
Do you remember what it feels like
To see your possibilities expand?

(Or do you just sneeze - *damn pappus* -
and continue on your way?)

Can you see the smoke laugh
As it curls out of the chimney?
It seems that it ate too much wood today
As it meanders through the sky, thick and heavy.

(Or do you just frown and think of how you
just cleaned the soot yesterday?)

Did you watch the color bleed out from the world
And turn your insides monochrome and empty?
Or can you still see the colorful world
The way you could when you were three?

LA VIDA

The children play
In the dewy mornings,
Joy echoing in the stillness.
They are laughing away
Believing every season
Has the gentle warmth of spring.

They live in hell
But are too young to know
What this means.
Their presence swells
Larger with each grin -
The predators have taken notice.

For there are hunters
And these are the hunted
Who forget they are meant to cower.
Toward the light comes death's new masters -
From the spring of life
The red vida blooms.

KITSUNE

You must be the most notorious thief of them all,
Making us respond to your every beck and call.
But we find that we don't mind,
As the only voice we wish to hear
Is yours, unfathomably sharp and clear.

So don't run away, kitsune.

Take us with promises and take us with lies,
Ensnare our souls with your cold, lovely eyes.
We will love you and hate you
And give you every pleasure
If that's what it means to keep an uncapturable creature.

So don't run away, kitsune.

You are gilded in marble and adorned with power,
Witty as a scholar and pretty as a flower.
You know best that your body is only a tool;
You lie in some upper stratum,
Watching us trapped in your kingdom.

So don't run away, kitsune.

You will always be precious, you will always be rare,
You will always stand a step above the fanfare.
But still, the mortals, to your lilting voice will sway;
Know that we will follow you
Even if you lead us astray.

So don't run away, kitsune.
Stay.

THE NIGHTINGALE'S SONG

Through the darkness, the nightingale calls.
'Tis a cry of revolution
Against the waking order.

From high heaven the songbird falls
A maladaptive evolution
As her wings grow ever shorter.

Her throaty cry of pain appalls
Her kinsmen and companion.
For when did the nightingale lose her elegant voice of wonder?

It was when they drove away her audience
And stole all of her confidence.

GLASS HEARTS

My glass heart beats clean and pure,
Each thump a tinkling birdcall.
With such a beat, I feel secure,
With each beat, I leave reality's pall.

For this idealistic heart is young,
And hopes to change the world.
From night's dark belly it swiftly sprung,
And watched as the dawn unfurled.

For this glass heart has never known
What it means to have no light.
It has never heard the people groan
From cruel, earthly blight.

And this glass heart has dreamt of
Wanting more and having less,
Never understanding the burden of
Living through distress.

I must beware of my glass heart;
Or else it will tear me apart.

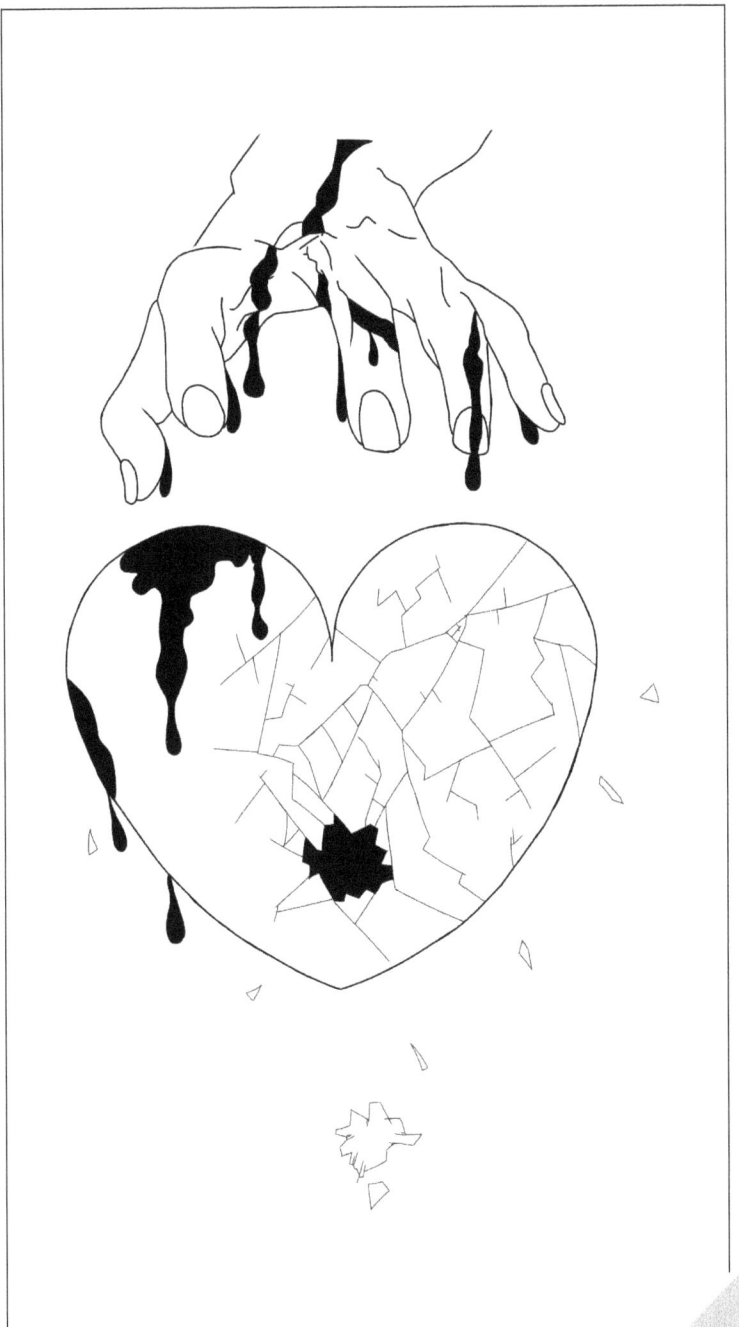

EDGE OF PARADISE

I have always dreamed of paradise,
With waves lapping at the shore -
A cliff at the edge of tomorrow,
And a view like never before.

And yet I stand with my back to the horizon,
And my feet rooted to the floor -
My only guidance are my stars,
My only faith is in lore.

At last - the sign does come one day,
A shooting star of hope -
And I know I will have someplace else to spend
The long nights with my telescope.

Slowly, chasing stars of glory
I see wishes crystallize -
And now there is what there wasn't before
At the edge of paradise.

EVIL JUSTICE

This city of fools
Wishes for a bloodless peace.
They throw away their powerful tools
And submit to the broken machine's artifice.

I will pledge myself to the revolution
Even if I must fight alone.
This is the only resolution -
I shall herald it as a king from his throne.

Do you balk at my version of justice
And fear the bodies strewn at my feet?
Know that this evil flower bloomed from your malice,
Watered by your approval, strange and bittersweet.

If these are my evils,
They are your evils too.

BETTER LEFT UNSAID

Each word spoken holds such power,
Swaying people, swaying fate -
Each letter a note of creation,
A strike of ink upon the slate.

But the silence behind the curtains
Pulls the puppet strings of noise,
Giving every word its meaning,
And every letter its poise.

There is the mighty roar of the exclamation
And the thought behind the comma -
There is the force of words omitted
From the vast plain of the manilla

So when a thought arises
Do not beat it till it is dead;
Think - will words do justice,
Or is it better left unsaid?

THE SPACE BETWEEN THEIR HEARTS

There's a place my parents have kept for me,
A place where I can be happy and carefree.
They are my teachers, my home, my happiness, my guards,
And I've grown up there, in the space between their hearts.

It was lovely and warm, and the air seemed to sing,
With the hope and joy of an eternal spring.
In this space I found comfort, and in this space I learned,
How to stand on my own two feet and
chase after what I yearned.

And now I will leave for a life of my own,
But that place will remain, the same as I've always known.
And even from afar, I will love them so terribly,
Because they are my parents, and because we are family.

COLORLESS TIME

The guileless white gives way to inky night
With nothing in between.
The silent writer sheds his ink upon the canvas
Staining it with sin on routine.

The silent writer spreads their lips
Paper-thin and white
And as their eyes follow me down the street,
Their gums are rotting and black and wide.

The silent writer made the clock
As deceiving as the rest.
The vast face sits, innocently eternal
But to the marching of colorless time, it is also behest.

The monochrome days will soldier on.
The monochrome people will follow.
And the monochrome clock shall lead them all.
Such are the days of the colorless time.

FIGHTING WITHOUT FIGHTING

There's never any fighting
Or hair-pulling or biting,
But there's tension nevertheless;
A great, heavy distress.

It settles over the spirit
Like a weighted, soggy blanket,
And crackles in the air
With nihilistic flair.

They shake hands, though it isn't true,
And smile because they have to.

They put angels on their faces
And devils in their hearts.

How do they stand it?
This fighting without fighting.

ALL TO SURVIVE

The spider monkeys shriek in fear
As the forest groans and clives.
Only yesterday, the possibilities were endless;
Now they only ask to survive.

The vipers hiss in anger
Watching the intruders arrive.
Yesterday, they were the rulers of this kingdom;
Now they only ask to survive.

The insects tither their displeasure
And swarm, confused, from their hives.
Yesterday, their world was safer;
Now they only ask to survive.

The alligators hear the mournful cries
And back into the water they dive.
They leave the dying rivers in a sluggish haze;
Now they only ask to survive.

IF WE COULD TOUCH THE STARS

The stars have always called to me,
And I look up in return.
They stretch as far as infinity,
Each one a floating lantern.

The seraphs sparkle in divinity,
Each as bright as the sun;
They will float for an eternity,
Reflecting silvery and golden.

How I wish that they would take me
And burn away my human bars;
If only we could find felicity,
If only we could touch the stars.

LITTLE BOY OF THE WOODS

There was a little boy in the woods
Who loved his home, and lived on love.
He never needed and he never wanted, but always felt
That there were other things he was meant for.
He longed to visit the city, and loved it from afar -
Later, he loved it from up close too. He joined
The knights and served the king and got rich
And ran from fights and did everything
a respected boy should do.
And his heart broke a little each time, screaming
From the pain of growing up. One day
The king was threatened and the kingdom was taken
And all the knights were nowhere to be seen. The boy
Could run too. He could be smart and save himself.
So he did - he ran towards the king and did his duty
And his heart lived on forever.
What was he to do?
When there were things worth fighting for.

CHAIN PARADE

Everyday, these sounds do mock me,
Sounds of a Chain Parade -
As I do walk among the ghouls
Feet dragging with the weight -

And everyday, I must endure
The silence in my soul -
Though heart and mind do scream at me -
To hell with all control!

Everyday, I am forced to fight
A murderous crusade -
Against those who try to chain me
To bloody cavalcades -

Everyday, the sound of marching
Does leave me in a daze -
For who am I to stop the march
Of ghouls in masquerade?

The endless night and endless day
Bear witness to the truth -
That I will hear until I die,
Sounds of a Chain Parade.

PEAKS

The ice freezes in my veins
And nips at my heels
Trying to drag me down in chains
And turn my fire to chills.
But I will not be weak,
As however cold,
The mountain is worth the peak.

No obstacles can stand in my way,
My dreams too large to be stopped by these outcrops
And even in these nights when the snow tints gray,
All roads will lead to the top.
And I will not be weak,
As however cold,
The mountain is worth the peak.

As I scramble to the tip
I finally look down
And feel my resolve slip
At the sight of the small, dead towns.
I promised I would not be weak,
But the mountain was cold,
And was it really worth the peak?

But as I raise my head from the ground
I see the distant, burning dawn
And know that soon enough, more challenges will come around.

SHATTER

The cool breeze feels natural
And the grass is stained sepia.
With one swipe I can make real
What was once only an idea.

And every day is a new adventure
With no limitation.
But some days when I think of the future,
I wonder if it is all just an imitation.

For all its intoxicating wonder,
This place will always be stagnant.
With no newcomer and no absconder,
My oneness remains a constant.

I don't know how to leave,
But I don't know how to stay,
As this tapestry unweaves
From its glorious display.

Help me to dispel these fears
And reclaim this hollow body;
When the dream shatters,
Will you be there to hold me?

REFLECTIONS IN THE SHARDS OF GLASS

In reflections in the shards of glass
The memories seem to glow -
And even the sharpest do surpass
Today's unfailing sorrow.

The angels come to play their harps,
And consciousness wilts from the bud,
While unrefined edges - raw and sharp
Draw drops of crimson blood.

And then blood leaves in a frenzy,
Hanging victims like a noose -
And death reclaims with memory,
The bodies that life does abuse.

Those who have upon them
A shadow - by death cast,
The future does not threaten -
They need only fear the past.

REQUIEM FOR THE LIVING

The Dead are honored with Soulful song,
That the Living must lose to give -
The Dead are said to do no wrong,
Yet they destroy with their directive.

Break free of Heaven's puppet-strings,
Cut loose the ties of Fate -
For the present brings glad tidings
To those who Future cannot dictate.

So when song floats by on gentle wings,
Remember that Time is ticking -
When song floats by on gentle wings,
Sing the Requiem for the Living.

THE MAN WHO LIVES IN 403B

1/1
There is a man who lives in 403B,
And his mind is slowly slipping.
He sits all day on his balcony,
Whispering scattered thoughts into nothing.

2/1
There is a man who lives in 403B,
And today he told me he went fishing.
He says he didn't find the freshwater crappie,
But I think there's other things he's missing.

3/1
There is a man who lives in 403B,
Who wakes me at night with his screaming.
And though his "friends", concerned, come out to see,
They seem like ants smelling prey and swarming.

4/1
There is a man who lives in 403B,
Who lives for the April rain.
For he thinks he can sit under the old oak tree
Without people seeing his tears of pain.

5/1

There is a man who lives in 403B,
Who never seems to be in a hurry.
His head hangs low and his feet drag heavy,
And he makes the children scurry.

6/1

There is a man who lives in 403B,
Who feeds the birds as they encroach.
And though they take his food agreeably,
They flee when he tries to approach.

7/1

There is a man who lives in 403B,
Who watches as we laugh in the yard.
It's clear he wants to join us in our glee,
But fears facing our disregard.

8/1

There is a man who lives in 403B,
Who makes me want to scream in his face.
Why do you stand there, dull and empty?
Why do you tolerate this disgrace?

9/1

There is a man who lives in 403B,
Who withers with the leaves.
Whereas one falls in a fiery red flurry,
The other watches the passing seasons and grieves.

10/1

There is a man who lives in 403B,
Who never festoons for Halloween in the fall.
And though others decorate to varying degrees,
His apartment is the scariest of all.

11/1

There is a man who lives in 403B,
Hiding behind his curtains and lattice.
And though he has gone silent lately,
No one seems to notice.

12/1
There was a man who lived in 403B,
Who loved the world till his last breath.
But since the world didn't love him equally,
He tried to free himself from regret.

1/1
Today, a man moved into 403B,
With a scared and closed-off style.
And though - no, because - I used to ignore the man in 403B,
I went to welcome him with a smile.

THE SAME SOULS

Are we each a planet,
Pulling the other into our orbits?
Ranging in disposition from azure to claret,
Clashing as we leave our circuits.

Are we each the sun and the moon,
One giving light for the other to glow?
For as I retreat into my cocoon,
You reveal yourself, my brilliant shadow.

Are we each a whistling wind
Clashing in the eastern sky?
Through the air we swiftly sprint,
Towards the horizon, we forever fly.

Or are you and I two different things
Two souls that, for one body, quibble;
I, the figure that at the lakeshore, clings,
And you, the mirage that fades with the ripple?

TO EACH CITY AND BEYOND

We scribble our names into the side of the train
And giggle as we run away.
The engine bellows its goodbye as it leaves our domain
Proud and tall in heyday.

It will soon leave this country grass
And head to places unknown,
Where towers rise from cement to glass
And small suns always shone.

Perhaps our names will travel
Over a waterfall in the east -
With greens and blues brighter than in any book or model
Shrouded in damp, thick air and blissful heat.

Maybe the train will take them
To another town like ours -
Where children look on as the breeze flutters their hems -
Their eyes alight with innocent wonders.

Who knows where they will travel?
Going to each city and beyond.

WORLDS AWAY

I often wake up falling,
Frightened by the day
But my stories take me somewhere else -
Some place that's worlds away.

A place where suns are golden
And the nights don't feel so cold -
A place I have the courage
To act a little bold.

I often dream the falling leaves
Are fairies in disguise -
Shimmering like the embers
Of a phoenix about to rise.

Sometimes the stories help to keep
The fears locked away -
But other days it's the stories
That feel like they are worlds away.

TOMORROW

I've always been little more
Than a kid from the suburbs,
With a desire to explore
That nothing else perturbs.

Isn't it strange? I've always thought
That change was in my hands -
That I had a shot
To shake the sea and turn the lands.

Ahead, I'll keep pressing,
And my voice will scream
I want to be something!
I will always cling to my dreams.

For I tell myself each morning
That I will move past the pity and sorrow.
And I know without anyone telling
That only I can choose my tomorrow.

THE ASHES OF OUR WORLD

The arms and legs rain down around us
Fresh wounds still dripping scarlet -
Staining the white expanse of this innocent canvas
And revealing their harrowing secrets.

One day, the front will come crashing down
And then, it will be every man for their own -
For when they feel they are about to drown
Their agony is second to none.

Then the animals come out to splash
The canvas black with desperation -
Leaving nothing behind but carnage and ash
Until every survivor is an aberration.

When you cut off their limbs,
There are only the hunters and the victims.

LITTLE COOKIE GIRL

Everyday at 3 o'clock,
The little cookie girl would come.
And everyday she would ask with her cookies on display,
"Would you like to buy something today?"

Everyday at 3 o'clock,
The little cookie girl would knock.
In rain or sun, snow or wind,
She always waited, and she always grinned.

Everyday at 3 o'clock,
The little cookie girl would skip to the door.
And even though I never opened up,
She never lost courage, and she always showed up.

Everyday at 3 o'clock,
I could hear the little cookie girl hum.
They say she sold cookies, but I knew her ploy;
Her currency was in hearts and her goods were pure joy.

Everyday at 3 o'clock,
I knew the cookie girl would come.
So when the doorbell didn't chirp one day,
I worried about what might keep her away.

And I found out from her neighbor
That the cookie girl came by
To sell cookies and gather well-wishes
For her sick old grandma in stitches.

People said there was an anonymous
donor who saved the lady's life,
As the cookie girl came back one day, her granny good as new.
But as the cookie girl walked by in the sun's golden-yellow,
She always looked up and smiled at my window.

TEARS OF BLOOD

His lips always smiled, this sweet little boy -
He always stayed brave for me.
Now this was a boy who knew how to enjoy -
Leap past society's rules and fly free.

His eyes never cried, this sweet little boy -
They say he was so happy, he forgot to feel pain.
But every laugh was just a decoy
For his inner turbulence and strain.

They say the eyes are the windows to the soul,
But these windows just reflected lies.
Everyone thought he was in control
While his third eye cried tears of blood.

SILENCE

When she went in her sleep,
Doll clutched to her chest,
The shadows began to creep
In the silence.

The fire never crackled
And the sky never wept -
Her final breaths never rattled
In the silence.

There was too little time to understand -
Too little time to be afraid -
Of what would come after judgement dealt its hand;
We did not know of this silence.

There was only me and the reaper, each of us a witness
As I stood thinking in this nothingness -
She would never have wanted this -
This silence.

REDWOOD WINTERS

The naked branches quiver
In the crisp winter air,
And weight piles higher and thicker -
It is more than they can bear.

They bow their proud necks
And arch towards the ground,
Unsure of their next paychecks
And facing despair so profound.

Yearly, these winters befall
The redwoods, inspiring courage and dismay -
And yet they never fall,
For they know that spring is on its way.

BIG FISH

You are a little fish in a big sea,
Too small to swim against the tide.
And the others hunt you constantly,
So what can you do, but hide?

The silver salmon prowl silently
And crest the waves with ease.
You candle fish swim urgently,
But the chase will never cease.

I know you wonder as you go to sleep,
Why so small? Why so weak?
Well, i'll tell you what you know and have hidden so deep -
That you already have the answers you seek.

For the natural order is not without reason,
And the cuckoo's laugh can signal something new.
For if you catch the silver salmon,
You become a big fish too.

HYACINTHS AND JASMINE

Rays pierce through, sanguine and bronze,
And the quivering jasmine calls out her response.
As the world wakes and the sun dawns,
The jasmine awakes - Ra's garb, she dons.

The hyacinth sways, watching, lost in her grace,
As the winds whisper of an empty place -
The morning dew falls from his face,
Crying tears for one who may never meet his gaze.

But one day, she glances back as he examines,
His gaze, caught, sweet and clandestine -
As petals unravel, he dares to imagine
Purple and yellow bleeding, leaving no margin.

And how they rule their valley in the morn,
As high and proud king and queen sovereigns,
As they sway together in the dawn,
Hyacinths and jasmine.

REACH ACROSS THE DECADES

Secrets never stay hidden
And stories are meant to be told.
Someday, someone will mention
The buried tales of old.

And in these, history comes alive
To read our hearts and touch our minds.
In tales, the dead will always survive -
The past and present, this truth always binds.

They cry out to be heard
And feel once again.
And when our bodies are finally covered,
Once more, the story will begin.

As the river of time rushes by in cascades
Faces pass, illusory and black.
So I reach across the decades,
And someone reaches back.

TWO WORLDS

I am a child of two worlds,
One foot on either side.
And the crows cawing heralds
Their inevitable divide.

And as the twilight comes,
Their eyes shine bright with malice.
Vengeance lives in their souls and echoes through their drums
And bleeds through the wine in the chalice.

I wish they would stop fighting,
But what do I know?
Between the worlds I am passing -
I cannot share in their desperate woe.

But they forget there are no borders
And there never had to be battle.
They forget about each others' anxious mothers and fathers -
They forget they are all still people.

WE ARE KINGS

We raise our voices to the sky
And sing one melody -
How glorious is our history,
How glorious is our joy.

Our hands reach out to grab the sun
As it sears at our brows -
Yet our smiles never falter,
Yet our feet carry us on.

From our bodies emerges a blistering flame
That sets the world aglow -
For the fires in the ocean mirror
The fires in our souls.

Together, we look to the horizon
And throw all cares away;
For we are the masters of the wind -
We are the kings today.

ANYWHERE

They talk about how strange I am,
Only half a woman and half a man.
It is clear that I am not welcome here,
So I put my head down, pack, and disappear.

I travel the world looking for somewhere to be free.
There must be some place with others like me.
I find it watching a woman down her
alcohol - the whole large can;
Her husband is like a woman, and herself like a man.

They are building a new house together
With acceptance as their bricks and
sunny humor as their mortar.
His dainty fingers knit the cloth for their draperies
While she hammers away at the roof and exclaims
that he makes up for her deficiencies.

The townsfolk gather after dark in the square
With dances to exchange and stories to share.
The man and woman spin gaily with them all
Looking each one in the eyes and always standing tall.

The townsfolk all love them;
There is no sign that they would condemn
The spark that each one has for life
Or the ferocity with which they face all strife.

I know now that this place's existence is no strange coincidence;
It was built slowly and lovingly by this couple's quiet confidence.
Where can I go, where I can dare to live and live to dare?
Anywhere.

THE ONLY LOYALTY

They call me a traitor
And say i'm a monster,
Because I once called their God
A fraud.

But tell me who is truer -
Those who follow an invisible saviour,
Or those who walk
Forward and forget the flock.

I stick to my ideals,
Not the symbols -
What else could I follow?
This is the only loyalty I know.

QUIET OUTSIDE

The storm kicks up inside my head
And blots out all the rest -
Through the din of the rising dread,
I hear them say that
It's quiet outside.

My pupils are blown wide but do not see
And my senses are all for naught.
And as they turn inward, slow and deadly,
I hear them say that
It's quiet outside.

Heartbeats echo in the silence
And lose their ebb and flow.
And in this dumb existence,
I realize that
It's quiet outside.

AS WINTER COMES AND GOES

The onset of winter appears harsher than ever,
And summer whispers its last goodbyes.
Snow swirls to the ground, coating the world
in white - first slowly, then faster, faster,
Tendrils of frost curl their cruel hands around the
thickest of trunks, pulling them to the ground.

The world is desolate and cold,
And not a living thing dares to peak its head above the soil.
Will the world ever live again, bursting at the
seams with bright laughter and simple joys?
There is hope yet - this at least shall never die.

Someday, the birds will sing their lovely
songs to the heavens again,
And hues of blue will meet lush green mountains on the horizon.
Every creature dreams of seeing an end to their misery,
But desperate months pass in silence as innocent
seeds lie in wait below the soft soil.

Finally, the snow melts, and the sun peeks
out from behind the clouds,
To see what has become of its beloved lands.
One small sapling lifts its head up in greeting,
Rising from the ashes of its predecessors.

Sun rays envelop the frost-bitten lands as they learn to recover,
And the lone plant grows - soon there are many of its kind.
When the next autumn comes,
The world does not shy away.

LOVE YOURSELF

The challenges of life have triumphed.
I do not think
I will have the confidence to love myself.
And when I ponder it, I realize that
The tiredness has seeped into my bones -
I know that in no way
Is the world being kind to me -
I must wonder
If this hard life is worth it -
And if I am making the wrong decision

(Now read it backwards)

DUALITY

These thoughts have spoken to me outright -
Crossed my mind
Till I cannot help but write
Of life's laws that lie behind.

They say they are the only verities,
And render me their fugacious captive -
Hold me in their entities,
And try to convince me of how to live.

But these ideas are not truths
And in this world of duality
We are the youths -
We choose our own reality.

ABOUT THE AUTHOR

Krisha Anant is a high school student who is passionate about science. When she is not writing, she enjoys drawing, dancing, playing violin, and spending time with her dog. Krisha lives in New Jersey. *Duality* is her first book.

Lightning Source UK Ltd.
Milton Keynes UK
UKHW010625020721
386516UK00001B/70